Bird Hospital
A & A Veterinarians
Franklin Square
437-7222

STARTING RIGHT WITH
LOVEBIRDS

STARTING RIGHT WITH
LOVEBIRDS

Risa Teitler
Professional Trainer

Photography: Glen S. Axelrod, 27. Herbert R. Axelrod, 31, 36. Michael Gilroy, frontis, title page, contents page, 6, 14, 25, 28, 32, 54, 62, 78, 80. Fred Harris, 16. Vincent Serbin, 19, 34, 35, 41, 44, 47, 57, 58, 67. Risa Teitler, 10, 11, 12, 17, 18, 20, 30, 37, 39, 42, 43, 45, 50, 56, 61, 64 bottom, 79. Louise Van der Meid, 9, 13, 21, 22, 26, 38, 48, 49, 52, 53, 59, 60, 64 top, 65, 66, 68, 69, 70, 71, 72, 73, 74, 75, 76, 77.

Some of the photographs in this book were made possible through the kindness of two Oregon lovebird breeders, James Brown and Darrol Grant.

ISBN 0-87666-557-1

t.f.h.

Distributed in the UNITED STATES by T.F.H. Publications, Inc., 211 West Sylvania Avenue, Neptune City, NJ 07753; in CANADA by H & L Pet Supplies Inc., 27 Kingston Crescent, Kitchener, Ontario N2B 2T6; Rolf C. Hagen Ltd., 3225 Sartelon Street, Montreal 382 Quebec; in ENGLAND by T.F.H. Publications Limited, 4 Kier Park, Ascot, Berkshire SL5 7DS; in AUSTRALIA AND THE SOUTH PACIFIC by T.F.H. (Australia) Pty. Ltd., Box 149, Brookvale 2100 N.S.W., Australia; in NEW ZEALAND by Ross Haines & Son, Ltd., 18 Monmouth Street, Grey Lynn, Auckland 2 New Zealand; in SINGAPORE AND MALAYSIA by MPH Distributors Pte., 71-77 Stamford Road, Singapore 0617; in the PHILIPPINES by Bio-Research, 5 Lippay Street, San Lorenzo Village, Makati Rizal; in SOUTH AFRICA by Multipet Pty. Ltd., 30 Turners Avenue, Durban 4001. Published by T.F.H. Publications, Inc., Ltd. the British Crown Colony of Hong Kong.

Peach-faced Lovebirds

Contents

Lovebirds can be very satisfying pets, if housed and fed properly. The first lovebird that you get may be an inexpensive Peach-faced or one of the more costly lovebird mutations that is being bred in the aviaries of American and European fanciers.

An important consideration before getting your first lovebird is whether it is the type of bird that you want. Lovebirds are an excellent choice for the beginning bird fancier, because their dietary needs are simple and the space required by them is fairly limited.

This book will give you a good idea of what a lovebird's personality is like and what you will have to do each day to keep the bird in top condition throughout its lifetime.

What kinds of lovebirds are there?

There are nine species of lovebirds that make up the genus Agapornis. These little parrots come from Africa, Madagascar, and a few small islands in the Indian Ocean. Some of the species are well known and distributed over a large area, while others inhabit tiny isolated regions and are rarely seen.

All of the species have basically green bodies and wings, but the facial coloration varies greatly. There are also bright colors on the breasts of some species. The beak may be bright red as in the Masked Lovebird *(Agapornis personata)* and Fischer's *(Agapornis fischeri)*, tan or beige as in Peach-faced *(Agapornis roseicollis)* and Grey-headed *(Agapornis cana)*, or black as in the Black-collared *(Agapornis swinderniana)*.

Some of the lovebird species well known in Europe, such as the Red-faced *(Agapornis pullaria)* and the Nyasa *(Agapornis lilianae)*, are rarely seen in the United States. The remaining two species of lovebirds are the Abyssinian *(Agapornis taranta)* and the Black-cheeked *(Agapornis nigrigenis)*.

The different species of lovebirds can interbreed. Crosses between the species result in *hybrid* offspring. Hybrids, the offspring of parents from two different species, are different from *mutations*. For example, a female Peach-faced Lovebird crossed with a male Masked Lovebird will have hybrid babies that show characteristics of both species but will not look exactly like either of the parents. In

Facing page:
A Masked Lovebird and a hybrid. Unlike some of the other lovebird species, Masked Lovebirds, due to their wide availability, are frequently seen in pet shops.

captivity, lovebirds of different species can be mated easily, but the birds must be watched carefully because some species are much more aggressive than others.

Lovebirds are small parrots with chubby bodies and short tails. Their total length is approximately five to six inches from head to tail. They have large beaks for birds their size, and some have rings of bare skin around the eyes (white eye rings).

Lovebirds are social birds; in the wild they live in large colonies. In captivity they can be kept in large groups also, but since they have a rigid peck order, they must be supervised. *Peck order* means that every bird in the group has a status relative to the others. The most dominant birds are considered to be at the top of the peck order. These birds can get away with pecking all of the other birds in the community; if they want to get to the seed dish, all of the other birds move out of their way. Lovebirds in the middle of the peck order can get away with pecking some of the other birds, but they must take a few pecks from birds that are higher in the peck order than they are. Birds at the bottom of the peck order may be pecked by all of the other birds in the group, but there are no other birds they can peck. Baby lovebirds start at the lowest part of the peck order and work their way up as they mature. If you have two lovebirds, there will be a peck order between just these two. If you have many lovebirds, it is important to get to know them well enough to identify the birds at the *lowest* part of the peck order. Each day, check to make sure that these birds are getting enough to eat and are not being pecked too much.

Whenever a new lovebird is added to a colony, it will automatically begin at the bottom of the peck order. Most new birds will establish themselves as members of the middle group within one day. You must be careful to watch the new arrivals to be sure that they are not injured by the other birds. Once they have established their social status, you can relax the supervisory watch.

Which lovebirds are usually available?

When you go to the local pet store and begin looking for a lovebird, you will probably see the following species for sale: the Peach-faced Lovebird, the Masked Lovebird, Fischer's Lovebird, and perhaps the Blue Masked Lovebird. The Blue Masked is a mutation of the Masked; its feathers are blue instead of green, but it is the same species of lovebird. There is also a Blue mutation of the Peach-faced Lovebird. Also fairly common in the retail shop is the Pied Peach-faced Lovebird. These birds look

Different lovebird species can be housed together. Here a Masked Lovebird of the Blue color variety shares its living quarters with two Peach-faced Lovebirds.

very much like Normal (wild-colored) Peach-faced Lovebirds, but have patches of yellow feathers on the breast, back, and abdomen. They are very attractive and usually more expensive than the Normal Peach-faced.

The price scale varies with the supply of lovebird species, but generally speaking you can expect to pay the lowest price for the Normal Peach-faced Lovebird. The Masked and Fischer's are slightly more expensive, and the Blue Masked still more costly.

When you begin looking at the other lovebird mutations, prices take a sharp jump, in some cases triple what the Normal variety costs. For example, there is a beautiful Yellow variety of the Peach-faced; like the Blue Peach-faced and the Silver Peach-faced, it is a very expensive bird. Prices are high because it is harder to consistently breed mutations with the desired coloration. It takes a long time to develop mutations into consistent strains, and breeders often spend many years perfecting a single strain. There is also a Silver mutation of the Masked. Fischer's Lovebird has a Yellow mutation, but it is very rarely seen in shops.

The type of lovebird that you get may well be determined by availability and cost. No one species is more likely to be

a healthy happy pet than the other. All of the species eat the same diet and require the same kind of cage. They are all very chattery birds but have limited speech potential. I have never owned a lovebird that talked, but I know people who claim that their lovebirds talk.

A cage should be large enough to permit a lovebird to stretch and exercise its wings. Cage location is also a prime consideration: a sunny windowsill is a suitable spot, provided there will be no *direct* sunlight.

How hardy and long-lived are lovebirds?

Lovebirds are very hardy birds, and with proper care they can be expected to live fifteen years or more. The main factors that affect the length of their lives are diet, genetic background, and environment. You cannot change the genetic background of a lovebird, but you can directly affect its life span by feeding it a diet of high-quality seed and the necessary supplemental vitamins and minerals as suggested in the section on feeding. In addition to the seed mix and supplements, you must also give your lovebird fresh fruit and vegetables.

Lovebirds rarely become ill when fed in the suggested manner and kept in clean cages with plenty of room to exercise. You must also be careful not to expose your lovebird to drafts, direct sunlight (which can dehydrate them), sudden temperature changes (such as may occur in the kitchen), or other birds whose health is questionable.

Compared to many members of the psittacine order, like the Salmon-crested Cockatoo, lovebirds are relatively small.

What kind of personality does a lovebird have?

By the time a lovebird reaches five or six months of age its personality has become well defined. For this reason it is far easier to tame a very young lovebird. An adult bird is a spirited, single-minded individual that very often is difficult to win over as a tame pet. Young lovebirds, although spirited, are much more flexible in their attitudes toward humans and will usually accept being handled. Most lovebirds acquired at a very young age learn to enjoy playing with you and will come to the side of their cage and chirp at you when you enter the room. They like to cuddle under your hand, against your neck, or in your hair.

Lovebirds are fearless individuals unafraid of dogs or cats or other, larger birds. I owned a lovebird that liked to fly over to my cat and land on her head. This usually startled the cat into jumping up and running away. The bird would then fly off and wait until the cat settled down somewhere else.

Besides being fearless, lovebirds are mischievous. They will hide in a fold of the curtains while you look all over for them. They will climb into your pocket or up the sleeve of your shirt. This mischievousness can get them into trouble unless you keep a good watch on them whenever they are

out of the cage. Lovebirds like to fly onto your head and play with your hair. They will fight with their own reflection in the mirror and try to beat up all of their toys. They constantly try to dominate everything.

I have never met a lovebird that wasn't a cheerful, chirpy little bird (unless sick, of course). While taking their afternoon naps most lovebirds tuck their heads under their wings and sing to themselves. Generally speaking, you can expect a lovebird to be playful, flighty, mischievous, and full of song.

How can you judge the age of a lovebird?

Most of the species of lovebirds available in a retail store look like their parents by the time they reach three and one-half or four months of age. There are some species, like the Peach-faced, that have slight differences in the color of their plumage until they are about four and one-half months old. With the Peach-faced Lovebird, a grayish face instead of brilliant peach is a sign of immaturity. Unfortunately, neither Normal nor Blue Masked Lovebird babies show differences in feather color from their parents. However, all species have black markings on their beaks

The black on the bill of this Peach-faced Lovebird indicates that it is still a youngster. Young birds adapt more readily to hand-taming than do adults.

when they are less than ten weeks old. These black marks on the beak are your best indication of very young lovebirds.

The eye rings can provide another sign of youth in lovebirds. Not all species of lovebirds have eye rings, but many do. When you see a lovebird with thick, prominent eye rings, it is already a mature adult. Young eye-ringed lovebirds will have very smooth, thin bands of skin around the eyes. The eye rings of young birds lie very flat against the face, while in older lovebirds they stand out.

Where is the best place to buy a lovebird?

The source from which you buy your lovebird is very important. Do not buy on impulse. Give the purchase plenty of careful consideration before getting the bird. Once you bring the bird home, you are responsible for its welfare and health.

Look around in all the local pet shops that sell birds. Almost every pet shop carries lovebirds, in addition to other small parrots. Compare prices, as well as accessories available (seed, cages, toys, books). The cleanliness of the premises, especially the cages in which birds are housed and the dishes from which they eat, is an important factor. Talk to the pet-shop employees to find out if they can answer your questions satisfactorily. After all, the pet shop will be the handiest source for help if you encounter problems.

If you want to tame your new pet, you must be sure that you get a young bird. Don't rush into the purchase without looking for very young lovebirds in at least a few of the local shops.

Lovebirds, like most parrots, use their bills as well as their feet for climbing.

14

Maintaining a Lovebird

What do you need before you bring the bird home?

When you buy your first lovebird, you should have some basic equipment on hand at home, or else get it at the shop when you buy the bird. If the shop does not sell bird food (most do), be sure to get the food immediately from another source.

Bird food is freshest when bought at a pet shop or at a store that sells animal feed. If you live in the country, near an agricultural area, or near a race track, there will probably be a farm-supply or feed store near you. People who live in urban areas will not be able to find farm-supply stores, and should make a point to buy their seed from a local pet shop. It is not recommended that you get the birdseed at the grocery store, because it is usually old and lacking in important nutrients that can be found only in fresh seed. However, you will want to buy some fruits and vegetables at the grocery, because lovebirds do eat these products.

Besides bird food, you will need vitamin and mineral supplements for your lovebird. Your pet shop will carry a variety of different commercial brands for animals. Be sure to buy the vitamin and mineral supplements made especially for birds; there are different brands to choose from.

Your lovebird must have a suitable cage to live in. You will have to shop carefully for a bird cage. Look for one at the same time you are shopping for a bird. You may already have a cage that was used in the past for a pet. If the cage is in very good condition, go ahead and use it, but be sure to clean and disinfect it completely before putting a new bird inside. It is best to get a *new* cage, and there are many designs to choose from. Look through the pet shop's inventory and select a cage with the following features: unpainted metal bars (a silver or gold finish is fine); wire top, instead of solid plastic; a wire grille, removable for easy cleaning; a removable tray, either metal or plastic; large, hard-plastic seed and water cups (budgie-sized cups are too small); a swing; wooden perches, not plastic; dimensions no smaller than 19 inches square by 18 inches high (plenty of flight area for the bird to exercise in).

The list of features above will give you an idea of what a good lovebird cage is like. You may decide to buy a cage

Facing page: **In order to keep lovebirds healthy and in top condition, strict attention must be paid to their diet and surroundings. Only *fresh* seed, fruit, and vegetables should be offered, and only cages that are spacious and kept scrupulously clean should be provided.**

with a closed top or without a wire grille, but be certain that the cage you buy is large enough for an active bird that likes to flap its wings and jump around. The recommended features are a good guideline by which you can judge the available bird cages.

There are other pieces of equipment that you will want for your lovebird, but the basic necessities for the first day have been listed above. In review, these are: fresh, high-quality birdseed, fruits and vegetables, vitamin and mineral supplements, and a well-made, roomy cage for the bird to live in.

What other equipment is helpful?

Besides the necessities just listed, there are some other pieces of equipment that you may find helpful. These things can be bought after you have acquired the lovebird, which gives you time to budget for them.

One very useful item is a T-stand. Since lovebirds are small, you can use a table stand. Table models can be used only with small birds such as lovebirds, Budgerigars, or Cockatiels. A table model is far less expensive than a floor stand and can be placed on any flat surface large enough to support the base. The usual design has a round base made of metal, usually aluminum, set on four short metal legs. The T-perch extends upward from the center of the base approximately eighteen inches, and the diameter of the crosspiece is between one-half and three-quarters of an inch.

You may decide to save up for a floor model. These are great for all birds, large and small. The design of the floor stand can vary, depending upon the manufacturer. Some of the models are fairly inexpensive, while others are very costly. I suggest that you buy a simple one. A stand for a lovebird should not cost you too much because it does not have to be as sturdy as a stand made for large birds. Be certain, however, to test the stand's stability. You should not buy any stand (either a table or a floor model) that would tip over if something hits it.

The purpose of having a T-stand is to allow the lovebird a comfortable place to sit when outside the cage. You may find the stand very helpful in your efforts to tame a new lovebird. Also, the stand provides a good playground for the lovebird when a few toys are added. The stand is a safe place for you to leave the bird if you want to walk out of the room for a minute. Be sure not to leave a lovebird out of its cage alone for any length of time, not even on the bird stand.

A final note on bird stands: unless you intend to tame

Although the main ingredient of the lovebird diet is seed, do not neglect to offer fresh fruit and vegetables each day.

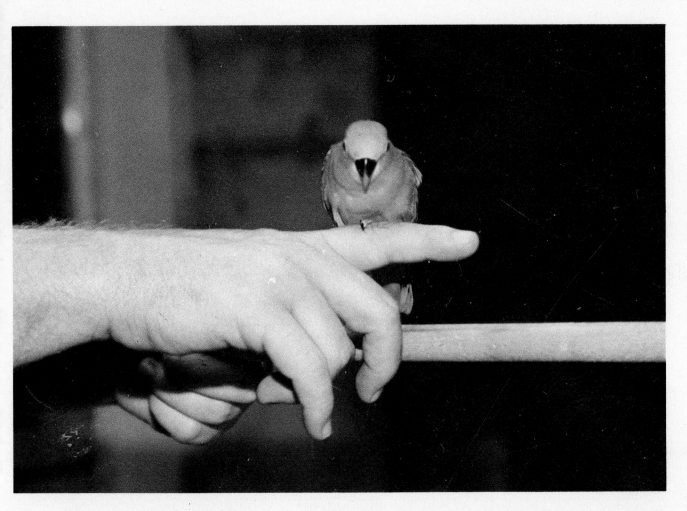

Once your lovebird has settled into its new home, you may want to hand-tame it. For this task, you will need a couple of training sticks.

your lovebird, the bird stand is not an essential piece of accessory equipment. If you do plan to tame the bird, you will find the stand extremely helpful.

You may want to invest in a cage cover. The cover should be made of material that will wash and wear satisfactorily for a long period of time. There should be no unfinished edges on a cage cover. All edges must be hemmed, or they will begin to fray after a few washings.

You should cover your lovebird's cage in the winter, when nights are cold. Very young or newly acquired lovebirds should also be covered at night. It is not necessary to cover adult lovebirds in the summer, but you can if you want to. The cage cover should also be used if you suspect that your lovebird is ill. Use the cover to keep the cage warm until you get the bird to the vet.

Extra food dishes may be necessary if there are only two dishes included with the cage. It is best to have separate dishes for each type of seed, one for water, and one for bird gravel—this means four dishes are needed.

If you plan to train your lovebird, you will need two or three training sticks. Training sticks are wooden dowels one-half inch in diameter, approximately eighteen inches

long.

A transport box is another good thing to have. You may need to move the bird in a hurry, and you should not have to waste time looking for an adequate transport box. The transport box can be quite small, unless you plan to travel a long distance with the bird. There should be small ventilation holes in three sides of the box. Be certain that the ventilation holes are not big enough for the bird to squeeze through. Good dimensions for a transport box are 10 inches high, 10 inches wide, and 8 inches deep.

What kind of toys should you give to a lovebird?

Lovebirds are very playful and thoroughly enjoy their toys. Buy only well-made toys. Look them over carefully before giving them to your lovebird. Although a lovebird is small, it can easily take apart any toy that is poorly made. Poorly made toys are dangerous to your lovebird, for they have sharp edges or pieces that can snag the bird.

Suggested toys for your lovebird include bells, ladders, swings, wood or rawhide chews, climbing chains, and mirrors. One of the all-time favorite toys for lovebirds is the plastic Kelly bird. A Kelly bird is weighted on the

Offer your lovebirds one or two toys at a time, instead of crowding their cage with too many. Lovebirds need plenty of room in which to move around.

Facing page: **Pet shops stock large, hard-plastic seed cups that fasten to the cage wires. The plastic material is easy to keep clean.**

18

bottom so that it cannot fall over. No matter how much your bird tries to knock it down, the Kelly bird will pop back to an upright position.

There are also food toys for lovebirds. The seed bells available at the pet shop are most common, but there are other food toys that you may want to buy occasionally. Keep in mind that the food toys for lovebirds have a very high calorie content. Many of them contain sugary binders, such as molasses, for the seeds. These are fine if given now and then as treats, but if you allow your lovebird to eat these food toys instead of its regular diet, your pet will become too fat.

How should you set up the bird cage?

When you first bring your lovebird home, you should set up the cage before placing the bird inside. Put fresh seed in the cups, after you wash and dry them. One cup should contain sunflower seed and the other Budgerigar (parakeet) mix.

Put fresh, cool water in the water dish and be sure to add vitamins. To determine the amount of vitamins, follow the directions on the package.

Ask your local pet dealer to assist you with the selection of a suitable lovebird cage. The size of the cage, which should be a minimum of 19 × 19 ×18 in., is important to consider, as is the material of which the cage was constructed.

One or two perches should be placed near the top of the cage, where lovebirds like to roost.

Locate the perches in the cage so as to give the bird room to move around without difficulty. Don't place perches above the food or water dishes, or the lovebird will soil the food and water.

You may want to put toys into the cage for the bird, but, as mentioned earlier, do not crowd the cage with them. Usually toys come with metal hooks to attach them to the cage bars. If you do not have hooks to go with the toys, get something to replace them at the hardware store. It is very dangerous to hang toys with string or thread. Lovebirds can entangle and injure themselves in string or thread.

Cover the cage bottom with newspaper or some other sturdy absorbent paper. You may want to use gravel paper that you find at the pet shop, but this is not necessary, especially since you should change the paper at least every two days. Gravel paper is expensive, and newspaper serves the purpose just as well. When using newspaper, it is not necessary to scatter gravel (also called grit) on the cage bottom. Gravel is best placed in a separate dish and given to the bird as a food supplement. You can put it on the cage bottom if you want to, since it is fairly inexpensive.

As with gravel paper, you may want to buy gravel covers

21

for the perches; again, this is unnecessary. If you provide natural wood perches, the bird's claws will wear down naturally, and you should never have to clip its claws. However, if you want to invest in gravel perch covers, go ahead. Be certain to change them periodically because bugs find the spaces between the perches and the covers a good place to live and breed.

It makes sense for large-scale breeders to buy various seeds in bulk and prepare their own mixtures. For keepers of one or two lovebirds, however, packaged seed is probably the answer.

Where should the cage be located?

After setting up the bird cage you should decide on a good place to put it. Try to place the cage close to the mainstream of family activity, such as in the family room. You will get the most enjoyment out of the bird if you can watch it while doing other things like watching television.

There are some places that you should not put the cage. Do not place the bird cage near steam or electric heaters. Make sure that the lovebird's cage is not near an electric fan or in the flow from an air-conditioner. Birds made to sit in constantly moving air currents can become ill. Even if you find it hot or cold, do not try to heat or cool your lovebird. Keep it in a sheltered spot and let it adjust to room temperature. Air-conditioning and heating by

22

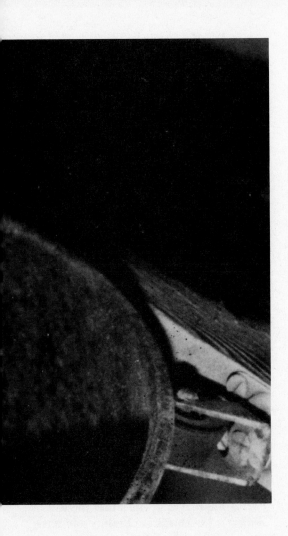

themselves will not harm your lovebird, provided it is not kept directly in hot or cold air streams.

Do not put the bird cage in the kitchen. Whenever the stove is used or the refrigerator door opened, the bird will be exposed to fluctuations in temperature. These temperature changes can also be the cause of illness in your pet.

You can place the cage near a window, if there is no draft in the winter, but never put the cage where it will receive direct sunlight. Direct sunlight, even for short periods of time, can dehydrate the bird and raise its body temperature above normal.

Placing the cage near a door to the outside is also unwise. Whenever the door is opened the bird may be exposed to rain, blasts of cold air in winter, or hot air in summer (if your room is air-conditioned).

Almost any other location in the house is fine for the bird's cage. Either hanging from a stand or placed on a table, the bird cage should be accessible for easy cleaning and servicing.

What do lovebirds eat?

The seeds your lovebird eats can be found at a pet shop. These include sunflower seed, budgie mix, spray millet, and hulled oats. The oats can be added to the budgie mix and fed in one dish. The sunflower seed goes into a separate dish, and the spray millet can be placed in the cage wire.

Lovebirds like to eat fresh apple and orange. You can also offer your lovebird raw corn, raw green beans, peas in the pod, and other fresh fruits and vegetables. Some birds will eat anything offered to them, while others are very picky eaters. Always give *raw* fruits and vegetables. Warm them to room temperature first, because cold food just out of the refrigerator can give the bird a stomach ache.

You should give a fresh leafy green vegetable to the lovebird every day. Use dark-green leaves from spinach, chickory, or romaine lettuce. Avoid iceberg lettuce, which has very little food value for the lovebird. Of course, you do not have to offer all of the above fruits and vegetables every day. Vary the items fed, offering two or three different ones every day.

Vitamins and minerals must be given to the lovebird to keep it healthy over a long period of time. Use a liquid vitamin supplement in the water cup every day; get one made especially for birds. Buy some conditioning oil to put onto the seed, such as cod-liver oil. Wheat-germ oil is very good also, but it is very expensive and may not fit into your budget. Use oils very lightly on the bird's seed. If too much is dropped on the seed, it will lump up, and your bird may refuse to eat it.

A mineral block rounds out the diet. You can buy a mineral block at a pet shop. Attach it to the side of the cage and replace it every few months.

What daily maintenance is necessary?

Once the cage is set up, you must maintain it every day. Developing a good routine of daily maintenance is the best way of protecting your lovebird's health. A good daily routine is easy to perform and takes a minimum of time. Try to attend to the bird cage in the morning. Make servicing the cage a part of your morning routine, along with washing up and dressing.

First, pull out the food and water dishes. Blow the chaff (seed husks) off the uneaten seed and add fresh seed. If your bird is a good eater, dump the whole cup and refill with fresh seed. Put the dishes on the counter. Cut a slice of apple or some other fruit and put it into the dish with sunflower seed. If you use a vitamin on the seed, such as conditioning oil, put just a few drops on. Now replace the cups in the bird cage.

Wash the water cup in the sink with warm water, using dish-washing soap on a sponge to scrub the sides of the dish. Rinse the water cup well to get out all of the soap. Refill it with fresh, cool water. Add the liquid vitamin that you use and mix it in. Replace the cup in the bird cage. Washing the water cup every day is very important. Although you cannot see it, there is a slippery film that forms on the sides and in the corners of the water dish each day. Be sure to get this film out before refilling the cup with fresh water. This is a good safeguard for your lovebird's health.

Wash a piece of green, leafy vegetable, then place it in the cage bars, near the perch. Give a fresh millet spray, if you have one. Wait until later in the day to give food treats.

After refilling the food and water dishes, you are ready to clean the cage. Pull out the tray and look at the debris on the paper. Check the bird's droppings. Look to make sure that the color of the droppings is all right and the consistency good. The droppings are the *best* sign that your bird is in good health, or the *first* sign of illness. Once you learn to recognize good droppings, you can check on the bird's health every day and catch any illness before it becomes too severe.

Look for droppings with a solid form to the white and dark-green (almost black) parts. The white is the urine in the bird's waste materials, and the feces are dark green.

Facing page: **It is obvious that these Fischer's Lovebirds are healthy and have been maintained with the greatest care. Both a nutritionally sound diet and a clean environment are important, as is a routine check of your birds and their droppings.**

24

When a bird is ill, the droppings change color and form. The normally solid droppings may become loose and watery. The color may change from dark green and white to orange, yellow, or brown. Black, tarry feces are also a sign of ill health. Whenever you find a lot of off-color or loosely formed droppings, be sure to consult a vet as soon as possible.

When changing the cage paper, you should also look to see if the lovebird has eaten its seed and vegetables from the day before. If you discover that the bird has not left seed hulls either in the dish or on the cage floor, watch carefully to be sure that it is eating enough. You can see why changing the tray paper is an important part of the daily routine.

If all is well, throw away the old paper and replace it with clean paper. However, if you think that the droppings look bad, keep a small sample of the paper to take with you to the vet. Try to take as fresh a stool as you can get.

The entire feeding and cleaning routine will take just a quarter of an hour or less. Remember, however, that this is only the *daily* maintenance and does not include the chores that must be performed periodically.

Perches will become soiled with bird droppings, so it is necessary to remove and clean them from time to time. After washing and scraping the perches, be sure to let them dry thoroughly before putting them back in the cage.

What chores are there besides daily maintenance?

Daily maintenance does not require you to wash the cage tray each morning. This is one of the chores that can be done less often but is just as important in keeping your lovebird healthy. Wash the tray at least once each week. Warm water and dish-washing soap on a sponge will do the job. Dry the tray, add clean paper, and replace it in the cage.

You should wash the food dishes every two to three days. Dry the seed cups very well before refilling. Wet corners in the seed dish permit mold spores from the dust in the bird seed to develop.

Every month sponge off the wires of the bird cage with fresh clear water. At this time you can also clean the perches.

How often can the lovebird take a bath?

In the warm summer weather, you can let your lovebird bathe every day, though it is not necessary. Also, bathing will harm the bird if it is not given at the right time of day. Be sure to give the bath early in the day. Morning is best, as this will allow plenty of time for the bird's feathers to dry out before sundown. Do not give the bird a bath on rainy days.

In the winter, when days are cold, give the bath less often. In fact, it is not really necessary for the bird to have a bath at all in cold weather. But if you have a healthy adult lovebird, a bath every two weeks cannot hurt it.

Do not give newly bought lovebirds a bath for at least one month. Be sure that the new bird is eating well and behaving normally before you let it bathe. Sick birds should not be allowed a bath.

You can buy one of the plastic bird baths available at the pet shop. These attach to the cage door. Fill it with water, and the lovebird will love to jump in and splash around. (The plastic bird bath is fine for both lovebirds and budgies, but it cannot be used with larger birds.) You can also let the bird bathe in a shallow dish of water placed on the floor of the cage.

Seeds are placed in seed cups, while vegetables (in this case, broccoli) can be fastened to the cage wires.

How do you identify a healthy lovebird?

You must know what to look for to tell whether a lovebird is healthy or sick. Healthy birds have clean plumage and all of their feathers. Dirty or shabby-looking feathers should alert you to possible illness.

Healthy lovebirds are active and noisy, jumping around and chattering to one another. If you stand too close to a cage full of untamed lovebirds, they will all crunch together in a corner. This is normal behavior. To see if the birds are active and chattery, you will have to step back and wait for a while to keep from frightening them. Once the birds get used to you, they should go back to their regular activites. If not, take a few more steps away from the cage or move out of sight.

Lovebirds have a four-toed foot. Look at the feet—legs, toes, and claws. If toes are crooked or turned to the side, there may have been a broken bone that healed. One crooked toe is not too bad, but don't get a bird with two or more missing or crooked toes. The skin on the legs and feet should be smooth and light pink in color. There should be no sores or lumps on the legs and feet.

Healthy birds have bright, alert eyes and smooth clear eye rings (remember that not all of the species have eye rings). If you notice any red spots or swelling on the eye rings, don't buy the bird. Also, look for any signs of watering from the eyes. If the feathers surrounding the eyes are wet or dirty, you should suspect illness. If there are two or more birds with wet or swollen eyes in the same cage, *do not buy any lovebird that is in that cage.* Eye trouble can be a symptom of many different illnesses, so beware of any lovebird with this condition.

Look underneath the bird's body at the vent. The vent is the opening through which droppings leave the body, and females lay their eggs through the vent. The vent area (the skin and feathers surrounding the vent) is clean in healthy birds. There is almost no noticeable opening when you look at a healthy lovebird. You can see the vent area by looking for the light colored feathers in the center and toward the rear of the bird's underside.

As explained in the section on daily maintenance, the condition of a bird's droppings is the best way to make sure that a lovebird is healthy. Check the description of good

Facing page: **Two Peach-faced varieties, a Pied Light Green and a Dutch Blue. Regardless of the species or color variety of lovebird you choose, all have the potential to be good pets. Just be sure to start with a healthy specimen, one that stands erect and alert, with bright eyes, clear nostrils, and smooth, shiny plumage.**

and bad colors and consistencies to determine if you are looking at healthy lovebirds.

Clean, clear nasal openings are another sign of good health in lovebirds. Clogged or runny nostrils are a sure sign of illness.

After making sure that the bird passes all of the foregoing tests for good health, you should try to feel the bird's breast. Take your thumb and second finger and feel the center of the breast. You should be able to locate the breastbone easily. When you do, touch it on either side with your two fingers. If it sticks out to the point that you can grasp it between your fingers, the bird is thin. Thin birds can be that way for many reasons. Do not purchase a thin lovebird. If you can feel the breastbone, but not grasp it, the bird has normal weight.

How do you choose a healthy young lovebird?

Once you have decided on a good pet shop, one that has a large selection of birds and accessories, you must choose one or two lovebirds out of the rest to take home. Using the descriptions already given of young birds and healthy and sick ones, you should be able to make a good selection. Of

Lovebirds are short, stocky parrots. Select one with a firm, well-muscled breast. Ask the seller to hold the bird you are interested in buying so that you can examine it for the signs of good health.

course, you will have to read these sections before buying the bird. It is recommended that you study the information available on the type of bird you want, to prepare yourself as fully as possible before you buy it.

What does a sick lovebird look like?

Sick birds perch with their feathers fluffed up (provided you are not standing too close). Both feet are on the perch, and they may have their eyes closed. They are quiet and do not interact with other lovebirds. They stay away from food and water dishes. Most of the time, a sick bird does not move from a spot on the perch unless you or someone else approaches the cage. With people close by, even a sick bird will try to move up into the corner with the other birds. The sick bird may have rapid or irregular breathing. The tail may move up and down with each breath. The nostrils and eyes may have signs of discharge or clogging. A sick lovebird is a listless, inactive bird.

Do not confuse a sleeping lovebird with a sick one. Around midday, most lovebirds take a nap. They tuck their heads back between their wings and chirp to themselves. There is one big difference between a healthy, napping lovebird and a sick one; healthy birds sleep perched on only one foot, but sick ones sleep on both feet. This is because sick birds have trouble with balance. Healthy birds are secure because their balance is good, so they don't worry about falling off the perch.

Do not buy a lovebird if you think that it may be sick. It is very difficult to treat a sick lovebird, especially if you have not done it before. Newly bought, untamed birds are even more difficult to treat for illness.

Are single lovebirds lonely?

Many people worry that if they buy one lovebird it will become very lonely or unhappy. I have never found this to be the case. A lovebird living by itself in a cage is usually a happy, active bird. A single lovebird enjoys attention from people more than a pair of lovebirds do. Two lovebirds will live happily together, but they by far prefer their own company to yours. Remember that a single lovebird may be difficult to pair up after it has lived alone for a number of years.

If your goal is to tame a lovebird, it is best kept singly. If the bird is given a cagemate, it will become attached to this companion and be less interested in you.

Taming and Clipping

Is it hard to tame a lovebird?

Speaking very generally, taming a lovebird is harder than taming a Budgerigar but easier than taming an amazon parrot. The difficulties that you will encounter depend upon you as a trainer, the way you go about taming the bird, and the bird's age. Although the personality of the bird affects taming somewhat, this should not be a deciding factor in your success or failure in taming a young lovebird.

You already know that an older lovebird will be far more set in its ways and therefore harder to tame than a young one, so if you really want to tame the bird, buy only a very young lovebird. Don't rush into the purchase, or you may end up with a bird too hard to handle.

Lovebirds are flighty little birds and full of energy. In the first lessons they will jump away and be almost impossible to catch, unless you clip the feathers on one wing.

Does wing clipping harm the bird?

Clipping the feathers of your lovebird, when done correctly, does not hurt the bird or harm it in any way. You can compare feather clipping to having your hair cut. You may not enjoy it, but it does not hurt. Looking at it another way, clipping the wing can prevent the bird from becoming injured. A fully flighted lovebird can fly straight into a mirror or window and give itself a severe head injury. Although it is true that a clipped bird on the floor can be stepped on if you are not careful, this is less likely to happen than the flying bird banging into something.

When the feathers on one wing are clipped properly, they will fall out and be replaced by new feathers in a short time. A clipped wing is not a permanent condition.

How often should you clip the wing?

A well-done clipping can last up to five months. If you want to keep your lovebird clipped, be sure to keep a close watch on its feather growth. Some lovebirds may replace their feathers in just three to four months. You will find that one day the bird does not fly, but the next day it does. Be especially careful if you take the bird outside with you or if it is near a door to the outside. Lovebirds can be out a door faster than you can realize what has happened. The bird probably does not intend to leave its happy home, but

Facing page: **A Yellow Peach-faced Lovebird. An active, healthy lovebird probably never will need to have its beak or claws trimmed.**

33

the attraction of other birds, chirping outside and flying around in the trees, is irresistible to most birds.

There are many former pet lovebirds flying around communities throughout the world which have escaped without meaning to do so. Lovebirds are able to adjust to most outdoor situations and do not often perish after escaping. Escapees can be found flying with groups of other small birds, who show them where to find food and shelter. Their tough personalities do not make them easy targets for large, aggressive birds, and usually they can outwit their opponents.

The only time you should really worry about your escaped pet surviving is if it happens in the middle of winter. Even if you live in a cold climate, a lovebird that escapes in spring or summer has had time to adjust to the coming cold weather and should be able to survive the winter, provided it finds a well-tended bird feeder and a snug hole to sit out the cold nights.

Prevention is best. Check on feather growth every twelve to fourteen weeks. Once you know the approximate time it takes for your lovebird to replace its feathers, set up a regular schedule of feather clipping.

The breast feathers on this youngster are growing in. Birds used to being handled from the time they are nestlings will become tame adults.

Facing page: **Taming sessions began for this Masked Lovebird while it was still young and unafraid of handling.**

34

How do you clip the wing?

To clip the wing of a lovebird you need experienced help. Take the bird to the vet or to the pet shop, or, if you have a steady person to assist, you may decide to try clipping the bird yourself.

I do advise you to study the procedure completely before attempting to do it. If you are unsure about any part of the clipping, do not try to do it.

Only one wing on a lovebird should be clipped. Some people like to clip both wings, but I find this unnecessary. The first four feathers on the end of the wing should be clipped in half. Be careful not to clip the feathers too close to the wing. The next seven or eight feathers should be clipped about three-quarters of the way up toward the base of the feathers. All feathers should be cut straight across the shaft. A good scissors is perfect for the job.

Be sure to extend the wing and look at the quills of the feathers that you are going to clip. If the quills are dark, they may be new feathers and should not be clipped. New feathers have blood in the quill. It is carried there by a vessel that grows especially for the purpose of supplying the new feather with oxygen and nutrients. Once the feather has grown to its full length, the vein is no longer needed, so it dries up and stops bringing blood into the feather quill. These new feathers, called blood feathers, are a normal part of the growth process for all feathers in all birds. After the blood vessel dries up, the quill changes color; it becomes beige or whitish, instead of dark. It is very important to be able to distinguish blood feathers from old feathers. If you cannot tell them apart, do not attempt to clip the bird's wing.

What happens if you clip a blood feather?

When a blood feather is clipped, it will bleed from the quill. If the bird is in good health and you clip just one blood feather, the blood should clot by itself in a few minutes. However, birds with vitamin deficiencies may have blood that does not clot normally. In such a case, a clipped blood feather can cause your bird to bleed to death. This is very unlikely, but it can happen.

If a feather begins to bleed from the quill, put the bird back in its cage and leave it alone. Look in on the bird every three to five minutes. Check the cage paper to see how much blood has dripped from the cut quill. If there is a pool of blood on the paper and you can clearly see more dripping from the wing at a rapid rate, you must stop the bleeding.

Do not panic or treat the bird until you have waited at

The wings of this Peach-faced Lovebird have not been clipped. Such a bird is difficult to tame because it is capable of flying away from you, especially to high, hard-to-get-to places.

By clipping one of the lovebird's wings, you will interfere with its ability to fly. Several of the flight feathers on this young lovebird have been trimmed. Cutting the feathers is not painful for the bird.

least five to ten minutes. If the rapid flow begins to slow up, do not treat the bird. Grabbing the bird will frighten it and cause the heart to beat faster. A faster heartbeat means faster bleeding from the cut quill.

If the flow of blood is really fast and does not seem to be slowing down after ten minutes, get some hydrogen peroxide and dry cotton swabs. Put some hydrogen peroxide on a cotton swab, squeeze out the excess and press the swab against the bleeding quill. Hold the cotton there for at least five minutes before removing it. If the bird is still bleeding after ten minutes of pressing the wound with peroxide and cotton, you must pull out the feather. If you live near the vet or a pet shop, go there and ask for help. If you have to pull out the feather yourself, be careful to pull only the feather that is bleeding. Grasp it firmly and do not bend it. Pull the feather straight out. Do not twist it or pull it up or down. Be sure to pull it straight out.

Never pull out a bird's feather unless there is no other choice. You could damage the wing by pulling out a feather incorrectly. You could even break the quill below the skin line and then you will have more problems.

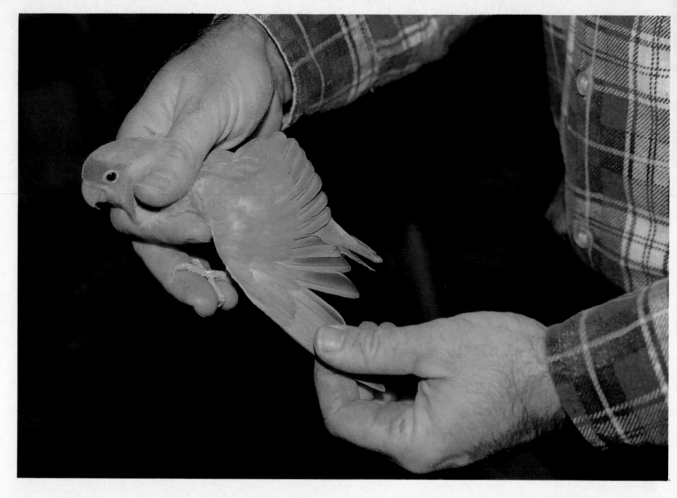

How should you hold the lovebird when clipping it?

Wrap the bird in a small towel or washcloth and hold it firmly, without squeezing it too hard. Hold the whole body and let the person who will be doing the clipping hold the wing. To prevent injury, the wing must be held at the point where it bends.

How do you release the bird after clipping it?

After the wing is clipped, you should release the lovebird either in its cage or on the floor of a small room (such as the bathroom). Hold the bird with its head up and its feet touching the floor or cage bottom. Release the bird's feet and then let go of its head.

The lovebird will attempt to fly off the floor. Expect this behavior. The bird needs time to discover that it can no longer fly. If you have clipped the bird properly, it will only be able to hop around on the floor, but not fly.

Should a lovebird's claws be clipped?

Most of the time you will not have to clip the claws of a lovebird if it has been given good, wooden perches to stand on. Natural wood perches are the very best that you can provide. On natural wood perches, the simple everyday

A clipped wing is not a permanent condition, as the clipped feathers eventually will be molted.

If you need to catch and restrain an untamed lovebird (or even a tame bird, for that matter), one way is to grasp it with a towel.

activity of moving around the cage will keep the claws trim. However, if you have kept your lovebird on plastic perches, or if you have bought the bird recently, you may find that its claws are too long.

A bird's claws are too long if they keep the foot in a cramped position on the perch. Overly long claws will not only cramp the bird's feet but may also lead to foot problems in the future. If you see that the claws wrap around the bottom of the perch, or if the bird's toes are kept up off the perch by the long claws, you should get the claws clipped as soon as possible.

What is the best method for clipping the claws?

Should you decide that the claws need clipping, you can take the bird to the vet or to the pet shop where you bought it, or to an experienced, qualified person who owns birds of his or her own. Never attempt to clip the claws by yourself until you have been taught how to do it by an experienced bird handler.

Claws can be either clipped off with a nail clipper (not a scissors) or ground down with an electric grinder. Most people prefer to clip the claws, because the tools needed are

39

much easier to acquire; electric grinders are very expensive.

To clip the claws, the lovebird must be held firmly to prevent it from moving around. You must also be prepared to treat bleeding from the claws, if it occurs. When claws are clipped too short, they will bleed, which is the reason for not clipping the bird's claws unless you know how to do it properly.

Each claw has a blood vessel running through its center. Unlike the vessel in blood feathers, these vessels never dry up and recede. In overgrown claws, the blood vessel may extend almost to the tip of the nail. In claws of the proper length, the vein comes to within one-quarter inch of the nail tip. Care must be taken not to cut into the vessel when clipping the claw.

If a blood vessel is cut by mistake, the bleeding usually stops by itself. However, in some birds the bleeding may be moderately heavy. In this case you must take action to stop the flow of blood as soon as possible. This can be done with the application of a styptic powder. Styptic powders are made especially to stop bleeding. Veterinarians have ample supplies of styptic preparations on hand. Pet shops usually do also.

The best advice for clipping the claws is to be quick and careful. While holding the bird securely, each nail of one foot is clipped, then the other. Each toe should be held separately as the claw is clipped. It is unnecessary to file the claws of a lovebird, because they wear down quickly after they are clipped.

Claws do not need to be clipped too often. You can put the bird down for its regular pedicure every four or five months.

Facing page: **The beak of this young Blue Masked Lovebird is normal; it is not overgrown. Active birds usually keep their beaks trim. In parrots, the upper mandible curves over the lower mandible, and this is why they have come to be known as hookbills.**

Should the bird's beak be clipped?

Some people say that clipping the bird's beak will reduce the painfulness of its bite. This is a very bad attitude. If a person is so afraid of a bird's bite that he feels the bird should be subjected to unnecessary anxiety, not to mention pain, he should not handle the bird. Better to leave it in its cage and appreciate it as a lovely creature than to disfigure it by trimming its beak.

The lovebird's beak should never be clipped or trimmed in any way unless the upper or lower mandibles are overgrown. You can be assured that lovebirds rarely have overgrown beaks. If you provide cuttlebone or mineral block, your lovebird will use it to trim its beak in a natural way and clipping will never be needed.

Badly overgrown beaks usually are a result of poor diet and the lack of essential materials for chewing. All parrots

require materials for chewing, such as mineral blocks, cuttlebone, and fresh branches. Overgrown beaks are easy to spot, once you have seen a normal lovebird. The biggest problem with overgrown beaks is that they can prevent the bird from eating enough food, since cracking seed may become a difficult chore.

If you think that your lovebird has an overgrown beak, do not try to trim it. Take the bird to your local veterinarian to have its beak trimmed. This is when the electric grinder comes in handy. The beak also has a blood supply, with not one vessel, but many. Cutting the beak is not as good a method as grinding it down, because veins may be cut too easily. The grinder slowly wears away the hard beak material. If the beak is ground down properly, bleeding rarely will occur.

How do you tame a lovebird?

To tame a lovebird, begin with a very young bird. You may want to wear cotton gloves, but this is not usually necessary. Work alone in a quiet room. Set the room up for taming in the following way. If there is no carpet, place a pad on the floor. If there is furniture in the room (try to work in a room with very little furniture), block the way

In order to tame a lovebird, you must work alone in a quiet area; speak in a soft, soothing tone of voice; and move slowly so that the bird learns to trust you and to feel secure.

Facing page: Lovebirds like to seek the highest perch; on a person, this is the shoulder or the head.

underneath with cardboard or towels—otherwise the bird will get under the furniture and be difficult to get back out.

The bathroom is a good place to tame a lovebird, but you should be sure to put away drinking glasses, razors, or anything else that the bird could get hurt on.

Bring the cage and a training stick into the room with you. If the bird does not want to come out of the cage when the door is opened, take a dry wash cloth and throw it over the bird. Using the wash cloth, lift the bird out through the cage door and place it on the floor.

Sit or kneel on the floor and try to get the bird to step onto the training stick. A training stick eighteen inches long is good. The diameter should be one-quarter to one-half inch. The lovebird will probably try to jump away from you at first. Be patient and move slowly. Place the stick in front of the bird and press it gently against its legs and stomach. Eventually, the bird will step onto the stick.

When it does step up onto the stick, sit still and let the bird rest for a minute. Then put it back down on the floor. Keep repeating this procedure, until the lovebird steps onto the stick every time it is offered. Talk softly to your bird. Remember that it is frightened and does not yet recognize

After the lovebird has mastered stepping onto the training stick, try teaching it to step from the stick to a T-stand. It will soon become used to the T-stand as a place on which to perch.

44

It may take a while to accustom your lovebird to being touched, but when the bird does get used to perching on your hand, slowly lower your free hand over the bird and stroke its head and back.

you as a friend. Training the new lovebird to step onto a stick and sit there may take one lesson or it may take many lessons. Most young birds will learn this lesson in a very short time. Two to four days of determined training should be enough.

After you feel that your bird steps onto the training stick easily, try substituting your hand. Continue to work on the floor—remember that your clipped bird must be protected from injuries that may occur if it falls too often.

Put your hand in front of the lovebird. Slowly move your hand against the bird's legs and stomach, just as you did with the stick. Keep the stick with you, in case the bird is stubborn about stepping onto your hand. If it is stubborn, use the stick to get the bird to step up. Then angle the stick toward the floor. The diagonal position will encourage the lovebird to climb upward toward your hand. Use your other hand to make the bird move toward the hand holding the stick. Move very slowly.

Hand-taming the bird may take much longer than training it to the stick. Keep working on the same lesson until you accomplish it. Even if the lesson in hand-taming takes three weeks or more, continue it on a daily basis.

Lovebirds like to cuddle. You may discover that your lovebird likes to cuddle into the palm of your hand. Go ahead and place your hand over the bird as it sits on the floor or on a stick. Do not pick it up, unless you put your fingers under its feet. Try to wiggle your fingers under the bird until it grabs onto your hand.

If the bird sits quietly in your hand, put it on your leg and keep your hand over it. Make sure that the bird will accept your touching it with your other hand. Gently pat the bird's head and neck. Although this is not going to teach your lovebird to step onto your hand, it will improve your relationship with it. Soon the bird will learn to trust you enough to rest for long periods of time with your hand over it. You should continue the drill of teaching the bird to step onto your hand, but make sure to pet and cuddle it every day.

After a while the bird may learn to sit on your shoulder. If you have been cuddling it, you may discover that it likes to climb into your shirt collar and go to sleep. Lovebirds also like to sit on your head and play with your hair.

In a few weeks you should be able to establish a good, friendly relationship with your lovebird. You can then safely take it around the house with you. Once it is easily retrievable with your hand, either by its stepping onto your hand or by allowing you to pick it up, you can take it into the family room. You will no longer need to use a particular room for training.

Facing page: **This Masked Lovebird seeks companionship as it cuddles in the folds of the author's shirt.**

When should you use the T-stand and how?

The T-stand is useful once the bird has learned to step onto a training stick. Place the bird onto the stand with your stick and teach it to remain there. Every time the bird jumps off the stand, retrieve it with the stick and place it back on the stand. Soon the bird will accept the stand as a safe perch.

When the bird is out of its cage, you can use the stand to keep the bird out of trouble when it is not perched on you. It is a good platform from which to hand-tame the bird also. You may find that your lovebird has not wanted to step from the floor onto your hand. But when you begin using the T-stand, the transfer from that perch onto your hand may become a very easy lesson for the lovebird to learn.

The T-stand can be used as a playground for your lovebird. You can also place millet sprays on the stand to give the bird a treat when it is out of the cage.

Begin using the stand in the room that you use for training. When you begin taking the bird out of the taming

There are more color mutations of the Peach-faced Lovebird than any of the other eight lovebird species. Some of the more common mutations include Dark Greens (*above*) and Pied Light Greens (*below*).

Facing page: The Dark factor is evident in several of these Peach-faced Lovebirds.

room, have the stand ready for it in the family room. Place the lovebird on the stand with a millet spray and let it learn to sit there in the presence of other family members. These people can readily approach the bird as it sits on the T-stand. Likewise, the lovebird can look around and get to know its new surroundings. The stand can be a very useful item with a tame lovebird.

When can other family members begin to handle the lovebird?

Once the bird is tame enough to come out into the family room, other family members can begin to handle the bird. Let them offer the bird a bit of millet spray. All new acquaintances should move very slowly when approaching the lovebird. Fast movements will frighten the bird into jumping down from the stand.

Of course, you can let other people in the family cuddle the bird in their hands once you find that the bird likes it. But be certain that they appreciate what you have done to teach the bird its tame manners. Coach them, and then leave them alone to form their own friendship with the bird.

Are some lovebirds untamable?

The vast majority of lovebirds are tamable when a program of training is started with young birds. As the birds mature, they become increasingly difficult to tame. Lovebirds are reproductively mature at about one year old; they are adults at ten months.

You may find that your lovebird resists all your attempts to make friends. It may in fact bite you every time you try to give it a lesson. My recommendation for such a bird is to get it a companion and to let them live in a spacious cage. You can consider these older birds untamable, or at least not good candidates for taming.

Facing page: **Unclipped birds (*above*) that are given freedom outdoors may be difficult to retrieve; in fact, some may fly away, never to be seen again. Don't fail to be cautious just because most of the time a hand-tame bird will be content to perch on its keeper's finger (*below*).**

A large-scale breeder often will keep a number of birds, both adults and juveniles, together in the same flight for exercise (*above*), but he or she will separate pairs and place them in their own breeding cages (*below*).

Facing page: Some breeders find it useful to install automatic watering systems in their aviaries or bird rooms.

When will your lovebird need first aid?

A good lovebird owner should be prepared to give first aid if it is needed. First aid is emergency treatment for either an illness or injury and should always be followed up by a visit to an experienced veterinarian.

It is very important that you do not panic if your bird needs first aid. Remember that accidents can happen, and usually do when you least expect them—before school, on holidays, and on weekends.

What do you need for first aid?

There are a few very useful first-aid preparations that you can use in an emergency. The hydrogen peroxide that you find at the drug store helps to stop bleeding and disinfects cuts. A bird salve can be found at your local pet shop and kept on hand for scrapes and sore spots. You can buy an antiseptic powder to put on wounds after you have cleaned them with hydrogen peroxide, such as BFI antiseptic powder. BFI can also be found at the drug store. Cotton swabs are also useful in treating wounds.

All other medications must be prescribed by your veterinarian. Never try to treat a cold with a medicine that is meant for people or other animals. Your veterinarian has studied for many years to learn what is helpful and what is harmful to sick animals and birds, so trust your vet to give you sound advice on medications.

If your lovebird shows cold symptoms, give the following first aid. Cover the cage and keep the bird very warm. Shine a strong light on the cage and get a thermometer to measure the cage temperature. Place the thermometer on the cage floor and check it every hour to see that the cage temperature is 85-90 F. Put clean paper on the cage bottom so you can better check the bird's droppings. Call your vet and get the first appointment available. Do not disturb the bird until you are ready to transport it to the vet's office.

Give the bird fresh food and any treat that it especially likes. Make sure that it eats as much as it likes of whatever it wants. If your lovebird will not eat, do not try to force-feed it; force-feeding should be left to the vet. You could choke the bird by trying to force food down its throat.

Facing page: **A hybrid, the result of crossing a Masked Lovebird with a Peach-faced Lovebird. Chances are that if you start with a hardy specimen, with proper care it will remain healthy throughout its life. Prompt medical attention by a qualified veterinarian is important in the event your pet becomes ill or injures itself.**

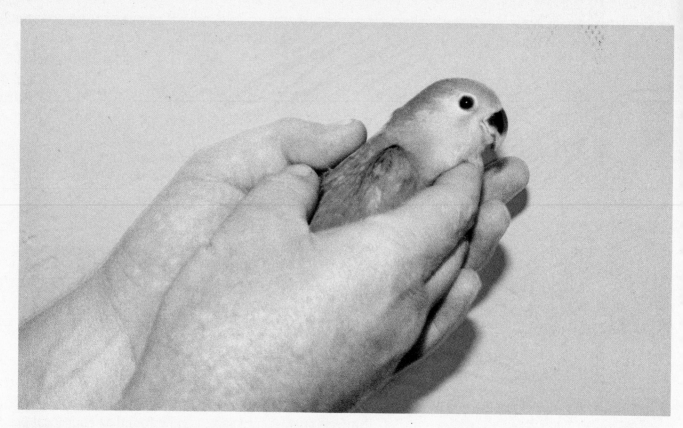

While holding your pet lovebird (*above*), you can give it something of a quick physical examination. Check the eyes and nares (nostrils) to see that they are clear and free of any discharge, and examine the bird's feet and claws (*below*).

Facing page: Check the condition of the plumage to see that it is free of feather mites or bald patches. This Blue Masked juvenile has had its feathers plucked by its parents.

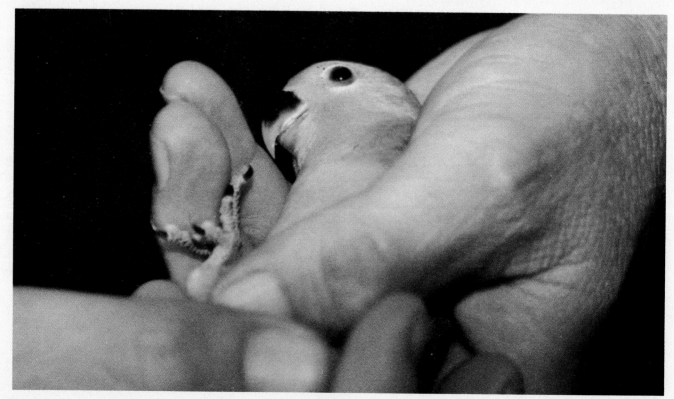

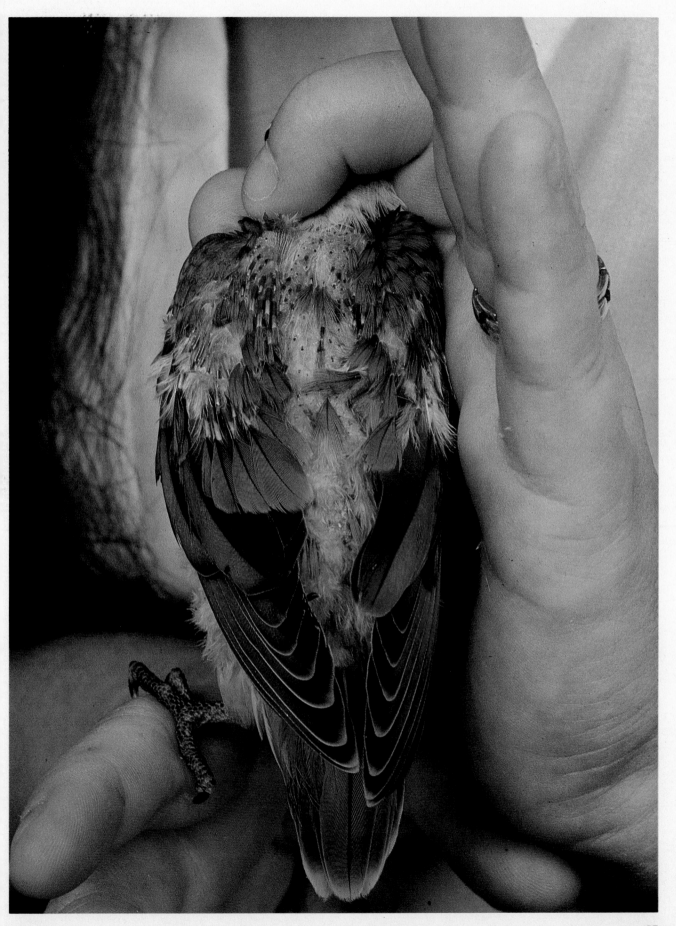

How do you take your bird to the vet?

When you are ready to go to the vet, put the bird in a small transport box, take a sample of the droppings with you, and keep the bird as quiet as possible during the trip. Recall if you have noticed any specific symptoms, such as sneezing, coughing, discharge from eyes or nostrils, wheezing, refusing to eat, and any others. Be certain to tell the vet in simple terms what symptoms you have seen and for how long.

Let the vet examine the bird and make recommendations for its care. You will probably be given some medication and directions for administering it to the lovebird. Before leaving the vet's office, be sure to ask any questions you may have. Follow his directions strictly. Take the bird back home and place it into its warm, covered cage.

Do not try to perk up a sick bird by playing with it. Let the bird rest, and disturb it only to change the cage paper and freshen its food.

Observe your sick lovebird, without bothering it, several times each day. Give any prescribed medications according to directions. If you have caught the illness in an early stage, you will probably begin to see improvement within

A really tame bird will not mind being held loosely in a cupped hand.

two or three days. Call the vet if there are any other complications, but do not take the bird back to the doctor's office unless he asks to see it.

How about accidents?

When accidents happen, they can be either minor or serious. First aid for minor cuts, broken feathers, or bumped beaks and eyes is mostly common sense. Put the bird back into its cage (the accident probably happened when the bird was out of the cage) and let it rest. Keep an eye on the bird for any signs of further injury. For these minor problems, don't medicate the bird in any way. Most of the time, if the injury is minor, birds will heal well.

Serious injuries, such as broken bones, must be treated by a qualified veterinarian. If the bird is bleeding heavily from a wound, you should get it to the vet, as soon as you have given first aid. For very heavy bleeding, take a cotton swab, dip it in hydrogen peroxide, squeeze out the excess, and press the cotton against the wound. Use enough pressure to keep the cotton in place tightly. Do not remove the swab for several minutes. If the bleeding continues to come through the swab, take a clean soft cloth and press it into the wound, leaving the swab in place. This should help to clot the blood. The lovebird should still be seen by the vet as soon as it is safe to transport it.

The best insurance for keeping your bird free from illness and injury is to take adequate precautions in its daily care and feeding. When you notice that a bird may harm itself by flying into a mirror, keep the bird away from it. Keep the cage clean and the food and water dishes well tended. Good maintenance is the key to a healthy lovebird.

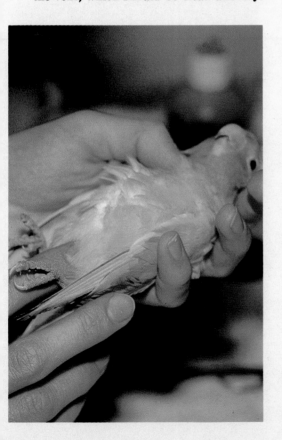

By blowing back some of the bird's breast feathers, one is able to examine more closely the underlying skin. One can also check the feathers surrounding the vent, which should be clean and dry.

All four of the white-eye-ring species, two of which are represented here (Fischer's and Masked), are closely related, as shown by their markings (*above*). The Blue Masked Lovebirds (*below*) exhibit the same markings as the Normal Masked Lovebirds, but the colors are different.

Facing page: A young Peach-faced perched in the foliage has not yet acquired its brilliant adult plumage.

Breeding Lovebirds

How do lovebirds reproduce?

Like all birds, lovebirds lay eggs, incubate them by sitting on them, and rear the babies until they are old enough to live on their own. A female lovebird that is kept by herself can lay eggs and may even sit on them, but these eggs will never hatch. It takes both a male and a female lovebird mating at the appropriate time to produce fertilized eggs. Mating must take place when the female bird is in breeding condition.

Sometimes two female lovebirds will nest and even lay eggs in the same nest box. However, the eggs of these two birds will not hatch, no matter how long the birds sit on them.

When is the breeding season?

In captivity lovebirds will breed at almost any time of year. Birds that live outdoors will adjust to the climate and enter their breeding season in the fall or in the spring. Often the breeding season is affected by the amount of rainfall in each year. There must be enough rain to assure the lovebirds the fresh green leaves and soft twigs and berries they will need to successfully rear their young. A good supply of fresh drinking water is also necessary for successful breeding.

Healthy, mature lovebirds will breed at least twice a year. Each time they breed, the birds usually produce a clutch, or nestful, of eggs.

How old do the lovebirds have to be to breed?

Lovebirds reach breeding age at about one year old. It is unusual for them to begin laying eggs before one year of age. Many birds wait until they are eighteen to twenty-four months old before they get serious about breeding. Once they begin the cycles of laying eggs and rearing young, they continue to breed for many years. Unless they overproduce, it is not unusual for lovebirds to continue breeding for eight to ten years.

Do lovebirds build a nest inside their box?

Lovebirds create intricate nests. The pattern depends upon the species. Different kinds of nests also result from the materials that are used to construct them. Nest building

Facing page: **Since Masked males and females look the same, and sometimes birds of the same sex will display affection towards each other, it is difficult to determine whether you have a male-and-female pair.**

63

A row of breeding cages (*above*), each of which has been furnished with a wooden nestbox, nesting material, seed dispensers, and water bottles. Often self-feeding youngsters are removed from their breeding cages and placed in a cage of their own. (*below*).

Facing page: In many breeding establishments, seed mixtures are often prepared in large quantities.

is a very important part of breeding. Constructing a nest is a stimulus to laying eggs. The birds continue to work on the nest while they lay the eggs and incubate them. They will also work on the nest after the chicks have hatched. Additional nesting material helps to keep the nest clean.

Materials used for nest building include soft twigs, leaves, palm fronds, and grasses. In captivity, the birds will use almost anything offered them, but often will not be able to build an adequate nest from paper or straw. Inside, the nest must be able to retain enough humidity and moisture; otherwise the eggs will not be able to hatch. The temperature of the air inside the nest box will seem warm and wet. These conditions are very important if the babies are to grow up nicely. Heat from the parents' bodies and the moist air in the nest benefit the chicks. Dry, cold nests will not sustain new life for long. Do not try to dampen the nest with water. The moisture must come naturally: from the materials used to build the nest and from the droppings and fruit that the parents deposit on the inside.

Both birds participate in nest building, but in some species the female does more work than the male. Peach-faced Lovebirds like to stick pieces of nesting material into

Lovebirds can be bred together in colonies, as well as separately in pairs.

Facing page: **Small-scale breeding can be done with a single pair of birds housed in a cage to which a nest box has been attached. Ventilation holes have been drilled into the nest box sides, and a sliding back door permits the bird keeper to occasionally check the nest to see all is well.**

With colony breeding, some breeders whitewash the front of the nest boxes in order to create a place for recording data (*above*). Record-keeping is especially important when dealing with varieties of a particular species. Below are two Dutch Blue Ino Peach-faced Lovebirds, the result of combining the Dutch Blue and Lutino factors.

Facing page: Sometimes the floors of flight cages and aviaries are covered with crushed corn cob for hygienic reasons. These particles help absorb moisture from the birds' excrement.

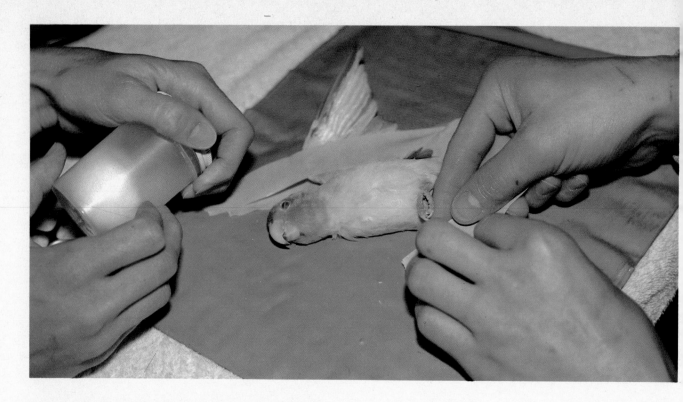

Visually, sex determination in some lovebird species is
nearly impossible because males resemble females. One way
to sex lovebirds is through laparoscopy, a method that can
provide certainty. A Pied Peach-faced Lovebird (*above*) is
restrained by having its wings taped prior to receiving
anesthesia (in this case, methoxyflurane by the open-cup
method). *Below:* Richard Hillmer, DVM, looks through the
laparoscope to identify the reproductive organs.

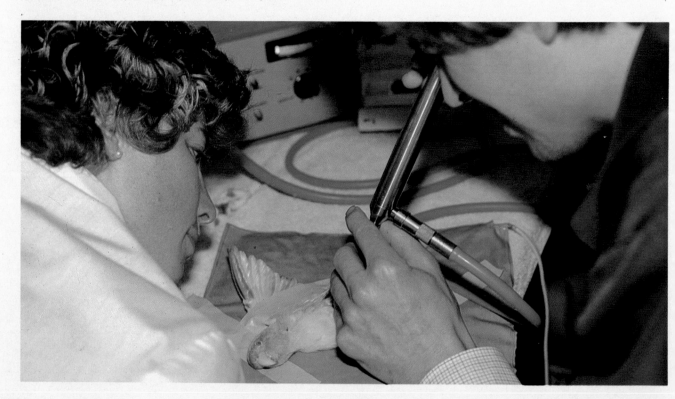

After sexing has been completed, Dr. Hillmer tatoos the lovebird's right wing to indicate that it is a male (*above*). The success of many breeding programs depends largely on pairing birds whose sex has been determined accurately. For some breeders, laparoscopy is an important tool. During the same visit to the veterinarian, a sample of the bird's blood can be taken to check its health (*below*).

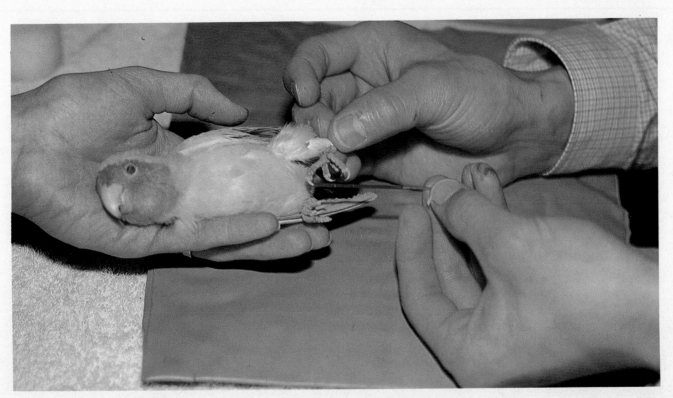

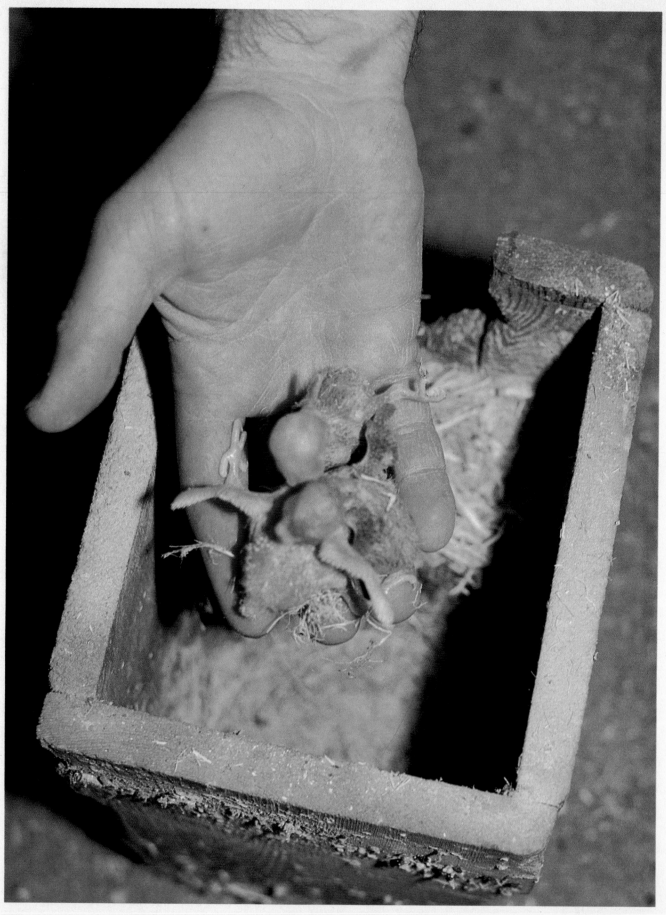

The eggs in a single clutch are laid and hatched at different intervals, so it is normal to find both eggs and nestlings together in the same nest.

Facing page: **These newborn chicks are flesh-colored and featherless. In several days their eyes will open.**

their back and wing feathers, but Masked Lovebirds carry material to the nest in their beaks.

How many eggs do they lay and how long is incubation?

The number of eggs laid varies from pair to pair. Some birds lay only two or three eggs, others as many as seven or eight. The number of eggs often stabilizes after the birds have been breeding for a few seasons. The average clutch size is four or five eggs.

Many times, not all of the eggs laid will hatch. Sometimes four or five chicks will hatch, but the parents feed only the three oldest babies. This is because they may not feel able to provide enough food for all five chicks. Instinct forces the parents to rear only the babies with the best chance for survival. Lovebirds will not spread the available food thinly in an attempt to keep all the chicks alive. They will choose the babies that they feel sure of raising successfully and ignore the others. This can't be called parental neglect, unless the parents stop feeding all of the babies. Even then, there may be very good reasons, from a lovebird's point of view, for not feeding the chicks. If the babies seem to the parents to have something wrong

with them, the parents may decide not to raise them.

The incubation period is approximately twenty-four days. It may be shorter or longer, depending on the climate and humidity outside as well as inside the nest. Incubation may not begin until after the second egg is laid.

Do both parents sit on the eggs and feed the babies?

Once incubation has started, the female lovebird spends most of her time in the nest box. She may come out occasionally to get a drink and eat some seed and fruit, but for the most part, she remains inside the nest, sitting on the eggs. Mating occurs often during the days when eggs are being laid, and the hen will leave the nest for mating.

At night, the male will either sit outside the entrance hole or climb into the nest and sit beside the female. During the day, the male will visit the hen often to bring her food or to place additional nesting material inside the nest.

Once the babies hatch, both parents feed them. The male does most of the work of feeding, until there are three or more chicks or the last egg has hatched. If only two eggs out of four hatch, the female will stop sitting on the unhatched eggs and help the male feed the young. The lovebirds may weave the unhatched eggs into the bottom or sides of the nest. They may even push the unhatched eggs

The flight feathers and tail feathers have emerged on these young Peach-faced Lovebirds (*above and facing page*); however, the feathers from the hindneck down to the rump have been plucked by the parents. Does one leave the plucked youngsters in their nest until they fledge, after which time the feathers will grow in, or does one remove the birds from their parents and hand-rear them until they are self-feeding? This is a dilemma that faces many lovebird breeders.

out of the nest entrance.

Although the lovebirds may stop sitting on unhatched eggs, the hen continues to spend almost all of her time inside the nest box with the young. The featherless chicks huddle together in a tight ball, and the mother sits on top of them. As the babies grow in size they also acquire feathers. During the first days, young lovebirds can double in weight in just twenty-four hours. In only four weeks they are almost as large as the parents. Many of their feathers have grown to full length and cover most of their bodies.

By the time the chicks are four weeks old, the mother is not spending as much time brooding them. She continues to spend a lot of time at the entrance to the nest. The babies are too big to sit on, but they cannot yet feed themselves. Both parents share in the work of caring for the baby lovebirds. Once the babies reach five weeks of age, they spend more and more time out of the nest. The parents want to coax the youngsters out of the box to face the world.

When do baby lovebirds leave the nest?

The chicks begin by sticking their heads out of the box,

A breeder extends the wing of one of his Pied Light Green Peach-faced birds to reveal the Pied markings.

76

Another Peach-faced mutation is evident here in these Pied Dutch Blue juveniles. This variety combines the Pied and Dutch Blue factors.

sitting jammed together just inside the nest entrance. Finally, one of the young lovebirds jumps out of the nest and joins its parents on a perch. Parents are tolerant of their chicks when they first leave the box, allowing them to run back inside if something scares them. When night falls, the babies sleep in the nest with the parents.

At six weeks of age the young lovebirds can be removed from the care of their parents. If there are two or three chicks of the same age, all three can be housed together in a separate cage.

Lovebird parents do not continue to tolerate their chicks for long after they leave the nest at six weeks of age. The parents are ready to begin the breeding cycle again, as soon as the young lovebirds can fly (the babies can fly when they leave the nest).

Repeating the breeding cycle (laying eggs, incubating them, and rearing the young), is called having a second clutch. It is possible that the birds may choose to have a third clutch.

How do the parents feed the babies?

Adult lovebirds eat their food and let it partially digest in

the crop. The crop is an organ in the upper part of the digestive system and receives food before it is passed on to the stomach. Digestive action in the crop prepares the food for the baby lovebirds. Liquid is added to the food, the temperature of the food increases, and then it is ready to be fed to the chicks.

The babies cry for food, and their parents respond by regurgitating the warm, liquid mixture into the babies' beaks. The mixture becomes less and less liquid as the chicks grow older. The parents begin to bring whole seed to the babies when they reach three to four weeks. They supplement the hard seed with soft fruit and vegetable foods.

During the weaning process, the parents feed less and less of the food from their crop and more seeds and fruits. In the course of two weeks the parents have stopped feeding their babies, although the chicks may occasionally cry for food. Sometimes an older chick will assist a younger chick by placing seed in its mouth. Very soon all of the babies can eat adequately on their own. By six-and-a-half weeks of age the chicks are eating independently.

What is egg binding?

Sometimes a newly formed egg becomes lodged inside the hen. The bird tries to lay the egg and may strain at it for over two days before becoming exhausted. In very severe cases, a female lovebird can die from egg binding.

What can be done to prevent egg binding? The answer is good diet and plenty of exercise. Sometimes a physical defect which is present can cause egg binding. In such lovebirds, egg binding will occur often, as long as the bird tries to breed. However, diet and exercise may help lessen the problem. Lovebirds that are well fed and get lots of room to flap their wings and jump around rarely suffer from egg binding.

Overleaf: **Fischer's Lovebirds.**